# TEACHING OF HISTORY SERIES

90 0053190 4

TELEPEN

This book is to be returned on
or before the date stamped below

UNIVERSITY OF PLYMOUTH

# EXMOUTH LIBRARY

Tel: (0395) 255331

The Historical Association, founded in
1906, brings together people who share
an interest in, and love for, the past. It
aims to further the study and teaching of
history at all levels: teacher and student,
amateur and professional. This is one of
over 100 publications available at very
preferential rates to members.
Membership also includes journals at
generous discounts and gives access to
courses, conferences, tours and regional
and local activities. Full details are
available from The Secretary, The
Historical Association, 59a Kennington
Park Road, London SE11 4JH,
telephone: 01-735 3901

The publication of a pamphlet by the
Historical Association does not
necessarily imply the Association's
approval of the opinions expressed in it.

# •*Contents*•

*Introduction* **Page 5**

*Historical Knowledge* **Page 6**

*History and Practical Wisdom* **Page 14**

*Further Benefits of Studying History* **Page 23**

*How and What?* **Page 31**

*Notes* **Page 43**

# *•Introduction•*

It is entirely appropriate — indeed it is the first element of what it is to be professional — that teachers should be able to offer justification for what they teach. It is sad, and significant, that so few teachers seem aware of the obligation, and fewer still to be able to discharge it. Particularly and most urgently is this true in the case of subjects under question or attack, given the fashionable clamour for 'relevance'. This paper is a modest attempt to fill the gap in the case of one such subject — history.

The quest for justification is really a search for a satisfactory answer to the question 'How will this study benefit the pupils?' *What* will they be able to be, or to do, having studied it, which they would not be able to be or do if they did not? And what grounds have we for thinking so? It is not claimed (of course) that this paper offers a comprehensive answer. Rather, it focusses upon one aspect believed to be crucial — namely that the question is fundamentally epistemological. There is no reliable way of estimating (and no convincing way of arguing for) the benefits likely to accrue to children from an experience except through understanding its nature. Some analysis of history as a form of knowledge is thus a necessary condition for any claim or statement, positive or negative, concerning its educational value. But two further questions arise. Supposing certain benefits can be shown to follow from the study of a particular subject; are those benefits only to be, or best, secured by that particular study? And are the benefits themselves important enough to take precedence over others which must be sacrificed if they are to be included? For whatever curriculum is chosen has an opportunity cost. Since it is, logistically, quite impossible for schools to include every study for which a case could be established, criteria must be found which enable choices to be made.

This second question is a problem — perhaps *the* problem — for curriculum theory, and as such really lies beyond the scope of this paper; for a full answer to it would involve a complete review of the nature of all subjects which are, or might be, included in the curriculum and the benefits (perhaps) to be obtained from them. Nevertheless the analysis of the first question — the nature of history — suggests that history is a distinct form of knowledge with correspondingly specific benefits to offer, and that these are so capital as to require making history a compulsory study for all pupils throughout their school lives.

# ●*Historical Knowledge*●

## Unique event: covering law: a resolution?

Traditionally there are two conflicting views of historical knowledge, that of the 'unique event' and that of the 'covering law'. According to the first, history is the record of an endless series of happenings, no two of which are in any fundamental sense similar. Historical knowledge is the recital of a mass of details — the 'explanation' of the French Revolution is simply an account of the sum total of events occurring in France between 1789 and (say) 1793 entirely separate from, and unaffected by, the consideration of any other events. According to the second view, historical knowledge is concerned with true statements which explain events by providing the necessary and sufficient conditions for satisfying and activating one or more general laws: explanation requires that events can be generalised into types because of fundamental similarities among them. We could not, it is argued, have such concepts, or use such words, as 'War' or 'Revolution' if this were not so. These mutually exclusive positions have led at least one authority to speak of the 'paradox of historical knowledge'. The present paper attempts a resolution of the paradox.

The argument is, briefly, as follows. The 'unique event' in the radical sense sometimes given to that term is a myth: the idea of general, or covering, laws or universals is an untenable exaggeration. History uses not laws, but law-like generalisations in order to give explanations: while it is true that they cannot help but use them, albeit tacitly, historians are not concerned to develop such generalisations; they are, nonetheless, inductively learned from the study of history: and despite their lack of full 'law-ful' status, they are neither obvious nor trivial. In fact their progressive elaboration and mastery largely constitute the whole frame of reference within which experience is correctly interpreted.

The premise which underpins the entire argument is that an historical narrative is *explanatory* and it must be stressed that this is not merely a contingent, but a necessary matter. The first reason why this is so is that a narrative is produced by selection and hindsight. In his penetrating exposition of this point, Danto invents an imaginary 'Ideal Chronicler' who knows whatever happens the moment it happens, even in other minds.

*He is also to have the gift of instantaneous transcription: everything that happens across the whole forward rim of the Past is set down by him, as it happens, the way it happens. The resultant running account I shall term the Ideal Chronicle (hereafter referred to as IC). Once event E is safely in the Past, its full description is in the IC*[1]

Danto points out that the first impression created by the existence of this Chronicle — that the historian's role is now redundant — is false. For, while it is true that he can by definition never improve on, or in practice even match, the comprehensiveness of the Ideal Chronicle's facts, 'the Ideal Chronicle will not tell him everything he wants to know'. For even the Ideal Chronicle can relate only events that were witnessed: and a great part of an event — namely, its consequences and general significance — cannot be witnessed because at the time when the event exists to be witnessed its significance lies in the future, and cannot at this time be known. It becomes known later to the historian by means of his hindsight, the probing, from his vantage point after the event, of its full significance. Explanation is retrospective. (Hindsight is further discussed in *How and What?* below.)[2]

This impossibility of correctly comprehending (as opposed to guessing about) the full significance of an event before its consequences have become clear not only makes hindsight a necessary condition of explanation but forces the historian to select among events and facts. For not all events have consequences, and, hence, significance. Many men, no doubt, died in April 1801; but it is the death of the Tsar Paul I which interests historians because of its great political importance, given the delicate diplomatic situation which it transformed. Many ships, no doubt, have been wrecked on the eastern coast of Greece by late summer gales blowing from the Black Sea; but it is only the occasion in 490 BC when the Persian invasion fleet was wrecked that interests historians, because of the ultimate contribution it made to an important outcome — the victory of the Greeks.

The tacit criterion employed for selection among significant events (as well as, to some extent, the decision as to which ones are significant) will reveal the historian's judgment concerning their relevance to whatever he is writing about. It is, of course, equally and reciprocally true that his particular account will be shaped by the facts of the case — his selection cannot be merely idiosyncratic — but that does not alter, indeed it strengthens, the present argument that the selection of facts is made in terms of the historian's wish to construct a clear account of some aspect of the past; and the fact that selection is made makes it an interpretative and explanatory account.

In constructing an account from the Ideal Chronicle, if he had it, or from the sources he actually has, the historian not merely selects facts as a pragmatic matter; he is driven towards a limited range of selections, if not indeed to a particular selection, by his (hindsight) knowledge that some of the 'facts' were fertile and others barren in consequences, and that of the former some, but not all, are relevant to the enquiry in hand.

The facts selected should, thus, be connected in two ways — each with its consequences, and each with every other fact selected because of their common relevance to what it is the historian is writing about. Such a selective principle must result in an explanatory narrative — in fact, valid criticism of it would largely consist of demonstration that the connections claimed are faulty, or that it ignored facts which have as good a claim to inclusion on the ground of their connection with what is being written about as some of those included. The point is that history is a record of change through time, and such a record cannot but select facts which were fertile with future consequences because they and their consequences are the changes which are to be recorded. In this important sense, Collingwood was right when he denied that explanation was some sort of additive to factual knowledge. When the historian knows what happened he already knows why it happened, because his narrative has selected among the facts he has surveyed in order to provide an explanatory account.

But of course a narrative involves more than facts. No deployment of evidence amounts to an intelligible narrative unless it embodies generalisations and sets of assumptions which, at the very least, are consonant with an adequately informed person's sense of probability. Danto[3] describes these generalisations and assumptions as 'conceptual' evidence and shows conclusively that an historical narrative is far more than a summary of the evidence which supports it. It is written — and the necessary selective process already described partly proceeds — in terms of concepts and assumptions of plausibility which enable evidence to be marshalled. Such a narrative is, of course, dependent upon its evidence — without which it would be pure fiction; but (short of just copying them out) there is no way in which an historian could use his sources except in terms of some such conceptual frame, for this is an indispensable means by which the selective process operates. Merely to classify an event as a 'war' or a 'revolution', for example, is to locate it under a concept and makes it plausible to apply a whole range of statements to it and to rule out other (logically possible) statements as inappropriate[4]

This is why the 'unique event' theory — according to which historians investigate a particular event oblivious of any question of its similarity to any other — will not do. For it really amounts to denying the use of conceptual evidence, as an example may make clear. Consider Christopher Hill's claim that under Oliver Cromwell 'The Protestant interest became once more an asset of English foreign policy'.[5] This might, at first sight, seem a rather puzzling statement. However, Dr Hill means that from time to time Cromwell used the antagonism of Catholics and Protestants in Europe at large to increase the influence and prestige of England by championing the Protestant cause. Dr Hill suggests that 'this was a purely nationalist policy'. When the role of champion could be expected to benefit England it was played: when it could not, it was abandoned. The key word is thus 'asset'. Ideological considerations, it is suggested, were no independent variable but were wholly subordinate to Realpolitik.

Now this must surely raise the question of how likely this is as an explanation; and while this may involve an evaluation of Cromwell's judgment, personality and temperament and will certainly require a close scrutiny of the particulars peculiar to the situation, fundamentally the answer depends upon whether foreign policy is likely to be conducted, and ideological weapons used, in this way. If no other instance in which this was so could be found, then belief in the explanation given would be weakened. In effect, then, tacit reference is here made to a principle of experience as to how foreign policy is conducted: the explanation of Cromwell's policy rests upon a general frame of relevant expectation in terms of which it is understood, of which it is an instance, and which, accordingly, it helps to establish and articulate.

In fact, of course, historians take it for granted that conceptual schemes exist in the minds of their readers which make their accounts explanatory: and these schemes can only come from experience, from knowledge that human beings in fact tend to behave in certain ways in certain sorts of circumstances. This must mean that the circumstances in question bear a paramount if partial resemblance to some which have existed on previous occasions. The whole notion of being able to explain any event at all necessitates the repudiation of its uniqueness if that term is so stringently defined as to exclude the possibility of comparisons as well as contrasts with other events. If an event really is *unique* in that sense, it cannot be explained. In the words of Sir Geoffrey Elton:

*As for history's preoccupation with the particular, that must be seen in its proper light. It is often asserted that the special distinction of the historical method is to treat the fact or event as unique. But frequent assertion does not create truth, and this statement is not true. No historian really treats all facts as unique; he treats them as particular. He cannot — no one can — deal in the unique fact, because facts and events require reference to common experience, to conventional frameworks, to (in short) the general before they acquire meaning. The unique event is a freak and a frustration; if it is really unique — can never recur in meaning or implication — it lacks every measurable dimension and cannot be assessed. But to the historian, facts and events (and people) must be individual and particular: like other entities of a similar kind, but never entirely identical with them. That is to say, they are to be treated as peculiar to themselves and not as indistinguishable statistical units or elements in an equation; but they are linked and rendered comprehensible by kinship, by common possessions, by universal qualities present in differing proportions and arrangements.*[6]

## Analogy, laws and frame of reference

'Unique events' then will not do as an account of historical explanation. But neither in its full-blooded form will 'covering law'. The frames of reference, or 'conceptual evidence', spoken of above are not the same thing as laws from which single conclusions follow ineluctably in particular enquiries by strict logical deduction. What history offers is really a series of analogies. It is never the case that events are exactly alike — how could it be? But this does not mean that different events may not be alike in respects which judgment and experience suggest to be particularly significant. This is how comparisons are made, and categories are formed. It is also what analogy is. Things are not analogous if they are identical.

But the process of comparison is not just a recognition of surface similarities. Analogy is really the exposure of *structual* similarity among events. Consider, for example, English/British involvement with the Low Countries. No details were common to 1585, the late seventeenth century, the late eighteenth century and 1914. The similarity was structural in the present sense given to that term — namely that no British government could tolerate the threatened dominance in Western Europe of any one power, particularly if this included control of the Channel approaches and coast. Indeed structural similarity is wider-ranging than this, in that analogy still operates even with fewer constant or common elements in the events which it groups. In the example, 'Ireland' could replace 'Low Countries', or 'Russia' and 'Eastern Europe' could be substituted for 'Britain' and 'Low Countries' without damaging the conceptual frame activated by the original pairing. Structural similarity is thus concerned with spotting and giving explanations in terms of analogous relationships between events widely separated in place and time, possessing perhaps no perceptually obvious common features.[7] Insofar as the reasons for the perceived similarity are understood, so that mere analogy deepens into genuine isomorphism, the explanation is strengthened.

Explanations are thus suggested by analogy which identifies circumstances in the case under consideration as similar or at least comparable to others already known and classified, and thus identifies the general 'law' or laws most appropriate to the case. But this reveals why 'law' is an inappropriately stringent term to employ, for it is important to remember yet again that analogy is not identity. Any two events with a structural similarity great enough to suggest analogy between them will also differ in other respects — in the personalities of their actors, for instance. This means that no event can be reduced to a standard case or instance of a completely regular process and cannot, therefore, be susceptible to, or manipulated by, laws. Such laws would require an invariant regularity of (say) political behaviour which is not to be found, and knowledge of particulars more comprehensive than can ever be had. It was not inevitable (logically deducible from any law) that Britain would go to war in 1914 in the way that it *is* inevitable that mercury will always expand when heated: it was merely probable that she would do so. Had it been inevitable because of the working of laws, why did — how could — the German government believe that British neutrality could still be secured even given the violation of Belgium required by the Schlieffen plan? And why did British public opinion have to be stirred by appeals to its general moral sense — the Prussian bully assaulting 'gallant little Belgium'?

The same argument holds if a wider perspective is adopted than that afforded by single events. Marxism, for example, sees the whole of human development as governed by iron laws of development which Man cannot escape. But even allowing for Marx's insistence on national differences, the record of change seems quite incompatible with the theory and the structure of alleged laws. Society in capitalist countries has not become more and more polarised between a more and more impoverished proletariat and a ruling crust of capitalists — witness the rise of the 'salariat' for example — and living standards for the masses have not fallen to subsistence level. On the contrary, they have risen. As to more international aspects, there is no sign of the Revolution in precisely these states where, on the Marxist dialectic, it should be imminent or already have occurred, whereas it, or something like it, has occurred in backward peasant countries where, on the dialectic, it should be impossible. Yet the revolutions that have occurred are quite explicable — those in Eastern Europe, for example, have little or nothing to do with the stage of economic and social development, but are a quite unsurprising result of Russian foreign policy — to be understood in terms not of laws but of law-like generalisations learned by analogy from the study of history.

However, certain dangers lurk within the process of thinking by analogies which are all the greater because analogy is so powerful. The essential point to be grasped is that analogy proves, and in a strict sense explains, nothing whatever; for it cannot build 'because' into the comparisons it suggests. 'Because' belongs not to the seriated instances which analogy suggestively links but to the reasons (if any) for that linkage which may subsequently be unveiled. The role of analogy is to suggest comparisons and similarities. It cannot rightfully be used to do more. Nevertheless, the fact that explanation is not a clear-cut 'present or absent, all or nothing' matter, so that it is not possible always to say whether a regularity is really explained or not, means that it is easy insensibly to pass over from suggestion to imagined proof and to conclude without more ado that an apparent similarity suggested by analogy is an actual connection. Suggestive comparisons must be most rigorously scrutinised for similarity before they are grouped under any generalised heading or any generalisation is built upon them.

Rightly used, analogy therefore forces us to focus on the particulars of the events compared and, in the light of this scrutiny, to determine how far, if at all, conflation under a generalisation is valid and, if valid, fruitful. In a word, it requires us to focus on the particular event. Applied to history, the significance of this is clear. It shows the intimate reciprocal relationship between conceptual frame and particulars by showing how the former reveal the meaning of the latter by classification, and how the classification is rigorously tested for appropriateness and validity by skilled use of the particulars. But, of course, such 'testing' presupposes that classificatory frames of reference are known. Both education and analogy thus fundamentally involve the use of the relevant general conception if it exists in the mind of the reader or pupil: its creation if it does not. Understanding grows from a multiplicity of analogous cases, each of which modifies or deepens the conceptual frame by the different chain of particulars it brings within it. And such a multiplicity of cases is to be found only in history, not only because the great bulk of analogous events lies in the past, but because the historian's knowledge of the outcome of past events, his hindsight, makes his account of them and his appreciation of their significance much more reliable than those of contemporaries distorted by unavoidable ignorance and confused by direct involvement.

This, then, is the distinctive nature of history, its unique contribution to understanding. It is unlike literature because, despite sharing the narrative form, its narratives aim to give true accounts of events which actually occurred. It is unlike the sciences which are law*ful* because their raw data, so to speak, are highly uniform. There is no need to inspect every sample of mercury to make sure that it is comparable to every other — that is known to be true and is the starting point of work. In fundamental contrast, history must focus upon, and rigorously scrutinise, particular events because human behaviour is too varied, and social circumstances too various, to be subsumed under laws. 'Laws' are not available; but without 'law-like generalisations' activated by analogy nothing could ever be explained at all. While it is true that historians, when pressed for deeper explanations, typically present more details of the particular event undergoing explanation rather than generalisation, law-like, or law-ful, this is not because they do not use law-like generalisations, but because their use of them is tacit. Only occasionally is it essential to state them formally in any but the later stages of education. To say of a move in foreign policy, 'Well — what would you expect? States *do* defend their interests' is useful only if the pupil is experienced and mature enough to know what sort of thing a 'national interest' is: and such understanding is to be had only from long experience, and many instances, of States actually doing things which he gradually comes to see, and to recognise, as 'defending their interests'. In short, the meaning and identity of the generalisation is inseparable from its use in explaining particular events which variously articulate it. A prolonged study of the historical record is the prerequisite for understanding.

# •*History and Practical Wisdom*•

## Prediction and anticipation

History, then, is a distinct form of understanding in that, while it cannot but generalise, the crucial need is to focus upon particulars from whose study patterns of partial similarity among events are tacitly discriminated, in terms of which explanations can be given. Analogy, albeit tacit, is thus central to historical explanation.

But while this account may establish the distinctive nature of history as a discipline, a question remains in terms of the programme outlined in the introduction. History enables us to understand the past. 'So what?' a sceptic might ask. 'It is the present and future which matter to our children.' The answer to this objection is implicit in what has been said, but it must now be made overt. Briefly, it is that analogy and the frames of reference built upon it project forward from the past into present experience, and when understood, may enable the outcome of contemporary events to be estimated. Does history enable us to *predict*? How far and in what sense?

A convenient starting point for the discussion is the argument of Hempel,[8] who maintains that the only difference between an explanation and a prediction is the purely contingent question of when they are made. A rational prediction could be made, and could only be made, on the basis of the known existence of particular antecedent conditions and relevant conceptual frames (or 'general laws' as Hempel calls them) from which a particular outcome can be logically deduced. In reverse, explanation can only be given in the same way. A result or outcome is explained if, and only if, it is shown to be the product of pre-existing particulars and general laws.

Now it could be argued that this asserted symmetry between explanation and prediction is supported by the nature of history. In constructing an explanatory account of (say) Bismarck's foreign policy does not an historian in effect predict? In showing how one step was followed by another he takes it for granted that this is not just a fortuitous succession, but that the first was a condition for the second — i.e. that given the first, the second could be predicted as 'likely'. If this is not so, then he has failed to establish a connection between the events, and has explained nothing.

However, this account overlooks an irreducible difference

between explanation and prediction. In Bismarck's case the historian's 'predictions' can be checked against — and are, of course, determined by — the known course which the event actually took, and the historian's knowledge of this — his hindsight — will not only powerfully affect the whole construction of his narrative but will influence the identity of the conceptual frame within which the narrative grows. The abundance of his empirical evidence is not only important in itself, but affects his conceptual frame of reference too. With prediction, however, this is not so. The empirical evidence is incomplete in that it stops short of the time to which the prediction relates. This latter rests solely upon the conceptual frame, activated by the (incomplete) particular evidence available and is of course quite unaffected by, and unable to take account of, further potentially relevant particulars which have not yet occurred.

The difference is thus between cases where hindsight is available and those where it is not, or to put it another way, between a case where the knowledge of relevant antecedent conditions is extensive enough for explanation to be given with confidence and one where this is not so, since what is to be 'explained' lies as yet in the future. Explanation is retrospective, and, because of this, particulars are available both to identify and to fill out an appropriate conceptual frame within which they build a logically valid chain of reasoning which constitutes the explanation. By contrast, prediction cannot mobilise a comprehensive supply of particulars, since it refers to a time which lies in the future. It rests upon a conceptual frame which is identified and filled out only tentatively by such particulars as are known at the time the prediction is made. In a word, prediction extrapolates from a conceptual frame — and from one which (compared to what is the case in explanation) is more or less tentative and indefinitely established because of the relative paucity of particulars available to identify and articulate it.

Is there, then, nothing in the 'prediction' claim? One element in the discussion must be emphasised before a final answer can be given. The similarity of difference between events is not just a matter of the frequency with which perceptually similar happenings occur: it is a matter of similar outcomes occurring for similar *reasons*. Historical scholarship, in the narratives it produces, tacitly exposes these reasons, and it is these which fundamentally constitute the frames of reference which underpin explanation. It may be that such understood trends can carry us beyond the present so that something of 'prediction' may be left.

Consider Russian policy in Europe during the last 150 years or so. Lenin's early insistence that the Revolution could not survive alone and the desperate efforts to foment a rising in Germany represented, in effect, an adapted version of the system of

Munchengratz. Nicholas I had then insisted that, if Russia followed an isolationist policy, 'the rampart against revolutionary doctrines would collapse and Russia could be obliged to grapple with France alone in a hand to hand struggle'. Just as Nicholas needed Germany as a barrier against French Revolutionary expansion, so the Bolsheviks needed her against Western, and particularly French, counter-revolutionary activities. Here, surely, underlying ideological, geographical and strategic realities are asserting themselves. In each case 'the true and permanent interest of Russia is to maintain between herself and France a . . . barrier formed by friendly powers based on priciples analogous to our own'. The same pattern is, of course, clear in the post-1945 position.

It is thus a fallacy to suppose that no antecedent causes of events which have not occurrred can ever be known. In the example, Russia with her immensely long and indefensible frontier, is, or feels herself to be, menaced; and she seeks to interpose between herself and her possible assailant 'a barrier formed by friendly powers based on principles analogous to (her) own'. It is predictable, given the facts of a long and indefensible frontier and a feeling of insecurity produced by this and accentuated by her sense of technological inferiority,[9] that Russia will act in this way whenever she is strong enough to do so with impunity or, at least, at a realistic cost. The obliteration of Poland in 1815 and 1939, intervention in Hungary in 1849 and 1956, the belt of satellite buffer states set up since 1945 and, finally, intervention in Czechoslovakia in 1968 (as well as the *coup* of 1949) seem clearly to bear out the argument. Given insight into Russian perceptions, which only historical knowledge can fully provide, the interventions in Hungary and Czechoslovakia, for example, as well as much else of Russia's post-war policy in Eastern Europe can not only be *explained* ex post-facto; they could have been *predicted* with reasonable confidence. It is clear that prediction is sometimes possible on the basis of understood trends, and since a trend involves development over time and cannot be studied in an as yet non-existent future, it can only be understood by a study of its past. In short, it is from history that understanding is to be obtained.

It is important to stress, yet again, the limited and modest nature of what this argument claims. In no sense does it endorse the strong 'covering law' position and in particular it repudiates that type of prediction which goes so far beyond analogical inference as to become prophecy, claiming to have penetrated, through historical study, to a set of laws which constitute a deterministic blueprint for the development of society. Such arguments ignore the fact, established above, that prediction can never rightly be as confident as explanation, not only because hindsight is not available to it, but also because, as was emphasised in the latter part of the first chapter, the great variation of human experience makes the idea of laws in this context almost inconceivable — if 'law' is meant in anything like the strict sense in which it is used in, say, the physical sciences.

It is, accordingly, necessary to distinguish a 'strong' and a 'weak' sense of prediction — between laws allegedly deduced from the past and binding upon the future, and law-like generalisations based upon events seen to be analogous through understanding of their causes which together make up frames of reference without which thought would be impossible.

In fact the distinction between 'strong' and 'weak' senses is so important, and so easily obscured, that it is better to forgo the use of the word 'prediction' altogether in connection with history. What the sense, gained from study, of 'how things are' enables us to do is to *anticipate*. It enables us to envisage a limited range of outcomes to present events as more or less likely to occur. It is in short the source of all rational expectation. No subject surely can have a stronger claim for a central place in the 'core' curriculum.

## History versus 'the past'

That its study enables us to make sense of contemporary events and in some significant degree to act intelligently towards them by anticipating likely outcomes, is the first benefit bestowed by history. But the argument is stronger than this. It may be possible to escape *history* (by knowing none) but there is *no escape from the past*.[10] As creatures endowed with memory our intellectual stance is ineluctably backwards-referenced. Each one of us has *a* version — some sort of version — of 'the past' which most powerfully, though tacitly, affects how we see present events. The 'present situation' in, say, Northern Ireland is not unambiguous or 'given'. It is something which has to be *estimated* and in that process of judgment our version of the (Irish) past is crucially involved. Historical study is by no means the only source of versions of the past. Before any history has been studied, the young child, in the process of socialisation, will have taken in, overtly and tacitly, a whole network of norms, assumptions and expectations; and in that network, interpretations of past events will powerfully figure. The version of the past which the child assimilates may be wildly wrong. In extreme cases it may be little more than a scream of fury and hate and fear, peopling the real present with bogeymen from a largely fanciful past. It may attest grievances, real enough, but caricatured by the myths which have grown up about them. But true or false, reasonable or unreasoning, thoughtful or superficial, it will colour perceptions of present realities and shape present attitudes and actions. If, for example, one's version of the past, however acquired, tells one that British policy in Ireland during the 1840s amounted to calculated genocide, then the version of the past which this view typifies will strongly affect how *present* events are seen and interpreted. The point is not that one, some, or any of these versions is entirely wrong or finally 'correct', but that according to which is believed current events will be differently interpreted — that is, beliefs about the past matter because they have present consequences. It is therefore of paramount importance that people's beliefs, and the versions of the past upon which they substantially depend, shall be as accurate as possible; and it is not to exaggerate, but simply to draw out the implications of what has already been said, to assert the superiority of historical accounts over other versions of the past.

But this claim must go beyond implication. In the previous discussion of the nature of historical knowledge, great stress was laid upon the most rigorous study of particular events. It is not suggested — in fact, it is denied — that such study will produce one agreed and 'right' account. History deals with matters that are essentially contested, and it is hard to separate facts and interpretations. But historical work involves the rigorous and conscientious study of 'what happened'. It is not informed and propelled by prejudice or by the desire to make propagandist points.

That may seem a large and even specious claim. But it is not some asserted impartiality on the part of historians as individuals which guarantees scruple and rigour: it is the nature of history as an 'open' enquiry which does so. The point is well made by Professor Hexter when he amusingly shows how the criteria of historical scholarship — 'commandments' as he calls them — are exercised by the whole community of scholars.

*The commandments are counsels of perfection, but they are not merely that; they are enforced by sanctions, both external and internal. The serried array of historical trade journals equipped with extensive book-review columns provides the most powerful external sanction. The columns are often at the disposal of cantankerous cranks ever ready to expose to obloquy 'pamphleteers' who think that Clio is an 'easy bought mistress bound to suit her ways to the intellectual appetites of the current customer'. On more than one occasion I have been a cantankerous crank. When I write about the period between 1450 and 1650 I am well aware of a desire to give unto others no occasion to do unto me as I have done unto some of them.*[11]

The validity of historical accounts is thus not dependent on the morality of historians, but upon their desire to survive professionally!

The 'interpretations' which make up such accounts cannot, then, be capricious or fancy-free. On the contrary they are constrained and shaped by the very 'frame of reference' discussed in the previous chapter. Since scarcely any event is unique, then no matter what event the historian is discussing there will always be other earlier events in some way(s) analogous to it. In other words the event is drawn within the 'framework of reference' which the study of history constructs and of which the historian, as a professional, is a practitioner. This will very powerfully affect how the elements of his event are understood and interpreted — he has a 'way of looking', a sense of 'how things are', a frame of probability, which determines how he sees 'the facts' and builds an explanatory account of them.

Of course the demagogue and mythologist, too, have a frame of reference into which facts are fitted and in terms of which they are understood; but it is not a frame of reference built on true analogies because it does not result from rigorous and critical scrutiny of particular events — that process which, as shown above, is built into the heart of historical scholarship. And the lack of critical scrutiny means that the facts themselves can be caricatured and even falsified.

Historical accounts of the past are thus doubly, and deeply, preferable to others. To explain events, historians draw them within frames of reference which historical study has produced, and which the newly explained events help further to articulate. Historical accounts are thus self-justifying by their achievement, to some significant degree, of truth. But in addition, they provide an antidote to the poison of mythologies, which may be literally murderous, manufactured from the prejudices of folk-lore — an antidote which consists of rational conclusions based on critical examination of evidence.

Indeed the superiority of, and need for, historical accounts is even stronger than this. It is usually not a question of combatting a complete and coherent, though mistaken or exaggerated, version of the past. More often there is no coherent version. This point is admirably discussed by Dr Kitson Clark[12] who describes the growth of the distortions of the past which shape men's behaviour in the present, Many of them

*may have been derived from confusedly remembered lessons learned at school, some inculcated by the reiterated assertions of politicians. Some associations survive from misty recollections of newspaper controversies, from scraps of special information or of personal experience, or the stories of chance acquaintances . . . [The result is that] . . . intelligent and apparently highly educated adults are curiously at the mercy of very questionable generalisations and descriptions against which any normal historical education should have guarded them.*

Dr Kitson Clark writes of educated adults, but the implication should be clear. What is involved goes far beyond 'getting the facts right' because one's frame of reference very powerfully affects how one sees the facts, and what facts one sees. The only adequate project is to combat the elusiveness of existing versions by challenging the whole framework of assumption which underpins the sort of fictional networks described by Dr Kitson Clark. This cannot be done quickly, and the inevitable conclusion must be that history must not only be studied by all pupils, but studied for a long time. This point is pursued in *How and What?* below.

## Objections

(i) **History and the 'fallacy of induction'.** Two objections must still be met. The first testifies to discontent with an analogy-based frame of reference, and a hankering after a lawful one. It asserts that any other frame derived from the past, if it is intended to have any anticipatory role, is invalid; for there is no reason whatever to suppose that the future (which includes contemporary events, whose consequences have not yet worked themselves out) will be 'like the past'. In short, this objection holds that to use knowledge of the past in attempting to understand the present and short-term future involves the 'fallacy of induction'. A comprehensive treatment of this important logical problem is beyond the scope of this paper; but enough may perhaps be said to answer the criticism as regards the application of historically-derived conceptual frames to contemporary events.

What troubles the sceptic is that he can see no reason to trust past experience. But, we may then ask, what does he mean by a *reason*? What stronger ground could there possibly be for holding an opinion or trusting a procedure than that all previous experience suggests that it is valid? 'A logically entailed connection' he may reply. But that surely reveals either epistemological ignorance or unwarranted assertion. He is shown either to believe that all knowledge-claims are in fact logically deducted, or to be asserting that they must be if they are to be of any worth. In either event he must simply be unaware that most knowledge is not so derived, but is empirical, resting centrally on experiment, observation and experience. Stringently interpreted, his assertion abolishes as invalid not only all 'common sense' knowledge but that based upon understood trends and well-validated laws as well. For, strictly, he must view all these as tainted with the inductive heresy: there is no logical reason why the laws of science, for example, should continue to operate beyond this present moment: it is just so overwhelmingly probable that they will do so that their continuance is built into the network of central and unconscious assumption with which we deal in the world and without which we could scarcely think at all. True, they are not logically deducible; but this merely says that induction is not deductive, and does nothing to show that induction is invalid. The sceptic fails to allow that there may be different forms which valid knowledge-claims may take and that deductive entailment is not necessarily the only possible basis for them.

Certainly a logically entailed connection is stronger than an inductive inference: but if the former is not available as a basis for thought then it is not reasonable, but the height of *un*reason, to refuse to accept and use the best which *is*. The frames of reference built by analogy from understood experience provide the best available means of understanding, and appropriately responding to, contemporary events.

**(ii) Frame of reference and common sense** The final objection to the argument of this work is that 'frames of reference' is a grandiose title for mere common sense or general knowledge — that historical study may involve them, but is not necessary for their learning since they are part of what every intelligent person picks up as he matures. Sir Karl Popper, for example, argues that *those laws may be so trivial, so much part of our common knowledge, that we need not mention them and rarely notice them. If we say that the cause of death of Giordano Bruno was being burnt at the stake, we do not need to mention the universal law that all living things die when exposed to intense heat. But such a law was tacitly assumed in our causal explanation.*[13]

Popper's procedure is suspect since it involves an attempted *reductio ad absurdum* of the opposing argument by means of a specially chosen example; in fact, of course, it is not true that the 'laws' underlying historical accounts are always so platitudinous. But Popper's error is more fundamental than this. By the example he chooses, he implies what he does not prove — that this sort of trivial 'law' is typical of history. On the contrary exactly because it is part and parcel of commonplace knowledge it is common to all modes of discourse. Hence, unsurprisingly, it appears in history; but to conclude, as Popper does, that it is therefore typical of history (still less peculiar to it) is to use the selected example not to penetrate, but to sidestep, the very question which is crucial — namely the possibility that there may be other sorts of law-like generalisations used by historians which are not universal commonplaces and which are derived from the study of history itself.

The whole tendency of the present argument is clearly favourable to this view, but it can be empirically tested along with the claim that it is from history that the classificatory framework of conceptual evidence is derived. An experiment recently carried out by the author may be relevant here.

176 honours graduates representing a wide spread of academic disciplines, all of whom were undergoing a post-graduate course in

teacher training, were asked to answer a test on the Russian intervention in Czechoslovakia. The test questions were based upon a leading article in *The Times* newspaper and the graduates were asked to comment. The criteria against which their responses were scored were obtained from content analysis of both a scholarly Western explanation[14] and a Soviet account of the intervention,[15] together with a set of criteria provided by a specialist in international affairs (who knew nothing of the purpose of the experiment) after he had read through the test. The criteria so obtained were highly uniform and are certainly examples of the sort of assumptions which underlie historical accounts of international conflicts. If they are trivial or obvious, or merely general knowledge, then certainly these very highly educated subjects should be fully familiar with them, and should have no difficulty with the test. If, on the other hand, the (tacit) generalisations are learned from history, one might expect the history graduates to surpass the others in test performance.

The results were interesting. Very briefly, they lent no support whatever to the first claim — that the relevant concepts are trivial and readily available. The scores were calamitous. With a possible maximum of 50, the mean score returned was 5.91. Even more significant than the scores was the number of graduates (nearly one quarter of the sample) who did not really attempt the test, entering some response to the effect that they knew nothing of the matter, and felt unable to comment. The second, competing, claim was that the (tacit) generalisations involved are examples of the sort learned from history. The graduates included a group of historians and their mean score was 13.90. As no other subject-group achieved a mean score of over 6.00, the second claim would seem to receive modest support.[16]

To sum up: there is no real 'paradox' of historical knowledge: neither the 'unique event' nor the 'covering law' account of history is adequate. Both are in part correct and the two are, in fact, complementary. 'Covering law' and 'unique event' both appear, but in a muted form. Because history is ineluctably explanatory, general conceptual frames are essential, for nothing else can make particular facts intelligible; but this makes imperative the most stringent scrutiny of particulars as an antidote to the wrong interpretation of events. The notion of understood trends reconciles change with law-like continuities, for to know the reasons for a trend is to know the kind of circumsance in which it will continue or cease to hold, and understood trends and the law-like generalisations they embody are built up by analogy rooted in the study of partially similar events. Generalisations are often neither obvious nor trivial; and they are learned from history.

# •*Further Benefits of Studying History*•

## Understanding specific issues: debunking myths

History, then, is the source of the conceptual frames in which important aspects of experience can be rightly understood because continuities, partial but important, are revealed by its study. This is the main benefit of studying it. But there are a number of other related benefits and this chapter is concerned to identify them.

It is not only through a general frame of reference, a sense of 'how things are' that historical study is valuable. Many examples readily occur of how specific aspects of the present cannot be correctly perceived and understood without the relevant history. The present troubles of so many African states cannot be comprehended without, inter alia, an awareness of their colonial origins — how, for example, their present boundaries were largely fixed in terms of rivalries or agreements between European powers rather than any indigenous needs or realities; and the origins of the Asian communities in East Africa is relevant to the immigration debate. If expectations of major change in the USSR with the accession of a 'dynamic, young' leader (actually, older than was Lenin at his death) are to be at all realistic they must be tempered by a clear understanding of the nature of Party rule in Russia, and the obstacles posed to change by powerful vested interests. In such understanding the historical record is an indispensable element. So it is, to take a very different issue, to the appraisal of a major problem in the international economy — Japan's enormous trade surplus with Europe and especially with the United States. If pressure, particularly from Congress, for retreat into ruinous protectionism is not to become irresistible, Japan simply must import more. But merely to state that fact is not enough. What is important is to understand the reasons for Japan's export-orientated stance and the consequent difficulties which confront any government in the attempt to modify it. Such understanding cannot be had without the historical record of a poor country, technically backward and short of most important raw materials, forced to devote its very limited supplies of foreign exchange exclusively to really vital imports and to boost exports to the maximum extent — the annual rate of growth of exports has exceeded that of GNP virtually throughout this century.[17] The result of this, particularly in a society in any case heavily marked by consensual norms rather than precise legal demarcations, is a pattern of intimate local economic relationships — between manufacturers and component suppliers, for instance — which is very hard for a foreign firm to penetrate. To realise the nature of the problem is not, of course, to solve it: but without this realisation the problem cannot be realistically considered at all.

Care was taken in the second chapter to distinguish mere trends from understood ones and to show that an estimate of whether or not a trend will continue or even whether it really still operates must involve understanding reasons for its occurrence in the first place and the modifications which have marked its development. In most of the examples given so far continuing trends and still-operative conditions have figured: but the historical record, since it deals in understood trends, also exposes, and can correct, anachronistic beliefs — beliefs which have failed to adjust to relevant changes in circumstance and which accordingly may lead to inappropriate action in the present. Consider British policy in Ireland. The historical record suggests a number of reasons for Britain's involvement. First and foremost were strategic considerations (as we would call them today). From the time that Henry II intervened to prevent too powerful a state from growing up beyond his control, to the Second World War when the guarding of the northern passage to and from the Atlantic was, almost literally, a matter of life and death, the effects of Ireland's location has been a matter which no English or British government could possibly ignore. Then there was the Protestant landed interest, originally 'planted' as an instrument of control, but by the late nineteenth century a major impediment to needful change, particularly through its political power in the Conservative Party and the House of Lords. There was also an 'imperial' argument. Increasingly after about 1880 it became viewed as imperative to hold Ireland lest any 'slippage' there should encourage movements for greater or even total independence in the Dominions or India.

Of these three reasons the last has long since ceased to apply; the second, with the Protestant interest almost devoid of political influence in Britain, has changed in both nature and real power; and, while the facts of geography have not altered, radical changes in world politics make it most unlikely that the strategic threat to Britain could recur in its familiar form. The reasons for British interest in Ireland have changed. Of course, there is always a time lag before consciousness catches up with such changed realities and it is understandable, if sad, that the main parties involved continue to strike postures of growing and dangerous irrelevance. But the nature of the change — and, indeed, the fact that anything has changed — cannot be understood without the historical record which describes it. It is that record which must colour present behaviour if this is to be relevant to existing, modified realities.

24

The genetic element in understanding applies also to ideas and institutions. To understand how and why something came about and developed is a large part of understanding the thing itself. The nature, extent and exercise of Prime Ministerial power, for example, cannot be fully understood, nor — this is the important point — critically appraised, unless it is viewed in the context of the royal prerogative from which it has developed. Estimating the pros and cons of single-member constituencies and a 'first past the post' electoral system depends in substantial part upon understanding how and why the system grew and developed. It is a mistake to imagine such arrangements as 'given' in any way whatever, except that they are the outcome of particular interests and perceived needs. The real 'lesson', if that is the right term, is that Parliament is a developing institution which has always changed (albeit tardily) in response to changed conditions — and which owes its continuance to that flexibility.[18] It is crucial to remember that arguments for things do not always — perhaps do not often — appear on the surface. To focus merely upon a present perception of an institution or practice is to risk missing its whole rationale. The record of how/why is a record of change and development in response to shifting needs and interests. In a word, it reveals and records the *reasons* for which change has occurred and, thus, the reasons for existing practice. This record is neutral with regard to what ought now to be done. On the one hand, the continued existence of the institution signifies a successful process of adaptation so far, and might be thought to show the reasons for continuance to be good ones, not merely traditional: on the other hand, the fact that an institution has successfully accommodated to pressures and interests does not, without more ado, show it to be right or still sensible. Whether, and if so what, changes are desirable and practicable is not directly given by past experiences; it has to be decided in terms of one's perception of present reality. But that reality cannot be correctly perceived without its context, without knowledge of the process whose outcome it is. What the historical record does is to explain and describe an existing state of affairs and thus provide an *informed* basis for decision and present behaviour. It highlights the continuing need for critical appraisal by showing change to be intrinsic to existence and indicates the form and direction that 'appraisal' may reasonably take by showing the sorts of problem actually encountered in experience.

A further, related, benefit of studying history is the de-mythologising power of the historical record, not only in the large sense of replacing superficial or mistaken frames of reference with appropriate ones but in the correction of specific myths. For example, it is commonplace to cite some alleged achievement as having been accomplished by a particular means, and then to assert that therefore 'history shows' the means to be an appropriate way of achieving some present objective. In such cases the historical record needs most careful checking first for accuracy and then for anachronism. Is the alleged record true? If so, have circumstances changed in ways that make the means no longer appropriate or effective?

As an instance of the first point, it is part of folk-lore that 'votes for women' was secured directly by suffragette militancy. The historical record reveals this as a myth. The Representation of the People Act of 1918 was not the measure for which the suffragettes (or the suffragists) had fought, and probably had far more to do with the effects of war, particularly with women's contribution to the war effort, than with earlier militancy. Indeed it took the very form to which the militants had been most opposed, by being a general measure applying to both sexes rather than a Bill specifically for women only; and by fixing the minimum voting age for women at 30, whereas for men it was 21, it was actually less favourable to women than the universal suffrage offered by Asquith in June 1914, but apparently scornfully rejected by the Pankhursts on the above ground. It was not until 1928 that women received the vote on the same terms as men and this, when it came, had little to do with pre-war militancy. Yet the achievement of female suffrage is often held to show that 'violence pays'. In fact it shows that a claimed precedent and justification for a present action needs close scrutiny of the historical record if it is not to be, at best, unjust, and at worst, disastrously misleading.[19]

It will be clear that those 'additional' benefits of studying history are not so much additional to the principal one described in earlier chapters as developments of some of its facets. Together they give some idea of the sort of thing which may be meant and covered by a frame of reference learned from the past and necessary for correctly appraising, and acting wisely in the present. However, to prevent any possibility of misunderstanding it must be re-emphasised that, while historical perspective is a necessary condition for understanding, it is not claimed to be, alone, sufficient. Tacitly, this point has been made several times by the frequent use of phrases such as 'inter alia' and 'in substantial part', and in the Japanese example the interlocking of historical and sociological factors in the explanation should have been made clear. But the point must now be made overt so that the claim for history is not devalued or discredited by imagined inflation. What is claimed is that explanation and understanding have an ineliminable, indispensable genetic component which only the historical record can supply.

## History and integration

So far the discussion in this chapter has concentrated on the benefits of studying history as a subject in itself. But this genetic element in understanding spreads beyond this limit. It is highly significant that the phrase 'history of . . .' can be prefixed to almost anything, including the other subjects of the curriculum.

The stress laid earlier, in the first chapter, and briefly reiterated above upon 'know howful' teaching is not confined to history but applies generally. Of course, this is mainly a matter of direct practice and experience in the various subjects, and this must be taken as read in what follows; but to the penetration of a subject's procedural rationale and nature the historical record can, it is suggested, lend a valuable increment. Science provides a suggestive example.

Just as activity gives direct experience, so the history of science gives vicarious experience of the scientific enterprise and, in so doing, both makes more explicit the criteria which guided activity exemplifies and covers ground which could not be covered by activity alone. Manifestly, the pupil's direct experience of enquiry could not even sample what science has achieved, and understanding must surely receive a great boost from complementary historical description of the course of development, of what changes have taken place, and when and why. Conant, concerned with the problem of understanding the 'Tactics and Strategy of Science',[20] argues that of the two ways of probing into complex human activities such as science, the historical and the logical/philosophical, the former 'will yield more real understanding for nine people out of ten'. He is not alone in this view. Hutten[21] argues that 'the natural evolution of ideas, that is their history, is more important than their ex post facto logical analysis'. Conant goes on: 'I doubt if the philosophical treatments of science and scientific method have been very successful when viewed as an educational enterprise', and recommends a 'case histories' approach, meaning 'a close study of a relatively few historical examples of the development of science. These examples would be so chosen as to require little factual knowledge or mathematics, and would concentrate upon the growth of concepts and techniques, the relation between science and observation and experiment, and the interconnections between science and society'. A particularly good example is offered by Hutten. He shows how the Michelson-Morley experiment of 1881 was the culmination of 150 years of work, how it gained its significance from previous connected study and how the work of Einstein, in turn, rested upon this chain. Hutten (p. 3) stresses the importance of the chain: it is 'the integration, the consistency of a number of different experiments which makes us accept a theory. If we divorce . . . any experiment from its historical background, we fail to see the criteria implicit in scientific research'.

This example would clearly be too complex for any but

advanced classes, but the rationale of the scientific process can be equally well illuminated for younger pupils by well-chosen case-studies. An excellent example is provided by Lister's development of antiseptic surgery. It is one of many which, in their essentials, are not at all difficult to grasp. A skeletal account reveals the essential structure of scientific enquiry which may be schematised as follows. Problem: death from gangrene — tentative hypothesis for solution to problem formulated in the light of a unique assemblage from existing 'knowledge' — in this case a new and highly speculative 'knowledge-claim' (Pasteur); practical implementation of hypothesis in testable form (carbolic spray — work of Crooks); appropriate and relevant test — provisional conclusions, and further refinement.

Two points need to be made. First, the above (quite inadequate) skeleton needs to be built into a proper historical account, the two main elements of which are truth and context. The account must be underpinned by and grow out of what can be discovered from reputable sources of how Lister went about his work, and it must be set in its historical context so that the conditions actually pertaining just before and during Lister's work may be clearly understood. It is only in the light of such understanding that the case study with its wealth of graphic detail (which is so telling for younger pupils), can exemplify the rationale of valid scientific enquiry. Without it, developments are made to look both arbitrary and automatic. Even more important, it must be remembered that any historical account — not merely of science — is a 'tidied up' rendering of reality. As pointed out above, the incoherent and half-conscious process which creative thought actually follows, means that even the thinker himself could not give a literal account of it (which is just as well for, if it really were literal, it would be unintelligible!). It is in principle irrecoverable. The value of historical accounts is not the comprehensive record they provide, but the way in which they highlight the salient features of enquiry. It is only through actual practice that the pupils' experience of science can become truly authentic; but a most valuable, if not actually a necessary, complement to this is provided by historical accounts of what scientists actually achieved, and how.

But if, as seems to be the case, what is at stake is the logic and status of scientific knowledge, is this not a philosophical question rather than a matter of the historical records? The stress on history in this paper is believed to be educationally sound. Philosophy of science is concerned with a formal, systematic treatment, and this cannot usefully precede a thorough understanding of concete examples which such treatment presupposes and which it exists to schematise and summarise. As always for children, the concrete must precede the general and, provided that the historical record has been constructed with regard to truth and context, i.e.

provided that it is a valid record, pupils who have followed it will already tacitly know from the examples the principles which philosophical treatment formally presents. The overt role of philosophy of science in school, it is suggested, will be confined to the ablest and most mature pupils.

Science has been used to illustrate the value of the historical record as a 'dimension' of full and rightful understandings; but an analogous argument is likely to hold for other subjects. 'Man must measure' is the title of one historically-based work on mathematics, and the record of *why* Man must do this and how he learned to do so may be most helpful especially to those of us for whom the seeming irrelevance of any but the most elementary parts of mathematics to anything we might ever need or wish to do is a major stumbling-block to learning it. Analogous considerations will apply to almost any subject. The contribution of the historical record is ubiquitous.[22]

There is indeed a further general argument — namely that most serious studies are not entirely self-contained, but are in part social and even political activities. That social role and nature finds its most explicit expression in the historical record. Moreover, in the course of surveying that record it becomes clear that most activities are related to one another, and full understanding of any of them is not to be had without a grasp of those connections. Cubism is partly to be understood in terms of developments, technical and otherwise, within late nineteenth-century painting, and partly in terms of social developments external to art itself — for example, our altered conception of the mind brought about by new psychological theories; the atom bomb was the result not only of the growth of scientific knowledge but of the needs of war — the latter being an especially striking example of social need determining the direction of scientific effort; changes in modern transport cannot be attributed merely to the technical development of the internal combustion engine — on the contrary, that development was itself prompted by a social context to which it was united. In a word, no comprehensive explanation can be given in terms of crude teleological 'tunnels', but through a whole social matrix within which the full historical 'contribution' to understanding is to be found in all its complex interrelations.[23]

As a corollary to this it appears that the teaching of every subject should have an historical dimension. But, of course, the various subject specialists will not entertain this as their main objective and they will not, therefore, find it appropriate or practical to explore the whole, or even nearly the whole, range of connections between their subject, other subjects, and the general social context. It is thus suggested that a role of history should be to knit together and fully develop the various strands of explanation which other subject courses have partially (and, for their own immediate purpose, adequately) developed, showing the wealth and range of interconnections which exist among them, and placing the whole within the central theme of political, social and economic development — the theme of fundamental importance which will only be touched upon by the other subject courses. In this way the current objective of an integrated curriculum might be achieved while preserving the integrity of its component elements by basing it upon intrinsic connections rather than mere casual associations.[24]

# ●*How and What?*●

## 'Know how': sources: anachronism

Anyone who accepted the foregoing argument, even if only in substantial part, but still questioned whether history should have a central place in the curriculum could, at first sight, scarcely be understood. One would have to ask serious questions about what he meant by 'important', about what constitutes putting subjects into the curriculum for reasons, and, indeed, about what he could mean by having a *reason* for doing anything at all. One would have to ask whether he was really indifferent to the truth or falsity of beliefs, and to the disastrous practical consequences of at least some erroneous ones.

However, his position might be more reasonable. He might accept the theoretical argument, but be sceptical as to whether the potential benefits of studying history will be achieved in practice. And such scepticism might seem well founded. School pupils' experience of history seems often to produce only modest or insignificant benefits of the kind claimed above. The explanation must be sought in pupils' experience of history — how far do their lessons model and mirror the true nature of the subject? To answer this question, that 'nature' must be examined further, for only if the pupils study real history can the benefits suggested in earlier chapters be achieved.

Like all disciplines, history is marked by a distinctive 'Know that' and a particular 'Know how' — that is, it is concerned to produce true statements about a particular aspect of experience (the past) and it has developed and refined over time procedures of enquiry particularly appropriate for this task. What this entails for history teaching has been discussed in some detail elsewhere.[25] Essentially, the point is that unless the pupils understand the 'Know how' upon which the factual accounts they learn are based they lack the 'right to be sure' about them and cannot, strictly, claim to *know* anything. Particularly, since they do not understand the rationale and criteria of the procedures of historical enquiry, there will be no way in which they can build the reliable frames of reference spoken of above, for they will lack the means of differentiating scholarly accounts from propagandist ones. But that would be to lose the principal benefit of studying history at all. As a practical matter, over and above the philosophical argument, 'Know-howful' teaching and learning are imperative.

Indeed, this is entailed by that rigorous scrutiny of particulars which has already been insisted upon. For what this fundamentally involves is *reconstruction* of a past which has vanished save for traces of it which fortuitously remain: and 'Know how' is a shorthand term for the process involved. It is not suggested, obviously, that to teach the full range of historical skills is a feasible programme for school history, but four fundamental features can be experienced — and must be if what is studied is to be hisory at all. They are sources, context, empathy and imaginative inference. A brief discussion of these will indicate a model for teaching, building upon the theoretical argument of earlier chapters.

Obviously, any reconstruction must rest upon and exhaust, or representatively select from, the evidence available for the event in question. Unless this is so the 'reconstruction' will be either fiction or propaganda. But the nature and use of sources needs more discussion — indeed, this will largely cover the other three points.

It has become commonplace for school 'text' books[26] to include extracts from documents or other original sources in the seeming belief that their mere presence guarantees that genuine history will be studied. But, of course, what matters is how the extracts are used. Frequently they are mere cosmetic illustrations or repetitions of points made in the text to which they lend apparent, but spurious, support — since their own standing is not established or usually even considered. When more extensive extracts are examined, this often amounts to little more than a naive comprehension test with the extracts taken as objective statements of fact and merely rummaged for trivial details. Such crucial questions as 'who wrote this?' 'how did he know — was he in a position to?' 'what were his interests/assumptions/bias?' are rarely investigated — but if they are not, the sources are not really being used at all. And it is a mistake to believe that this cannot, in some significant measure, be done even with younger children. Consider this passage, one of many used in the 'Fermanagh project'[27] with 10 and 12 year-olds studying the Nine Years' War:

*For as Tyrone is the dishonestest rebel in the world, so is he the most cowardly, never making good any fight but skirmishing in passes, bogs, woods, fords and all places of advantage.*

The children in the Fermanagh project can readily be led to recognise this as no objective testimony but as representing an exasperated outburst from a particular point of view. They can certainly be led from this to *reconstruction*. They can *empathise* with the frustration evidently felt by the writer through their previously established knowledge of the logistics of the war — the difficulties faced by regular troops confronted by guerilla forces in terrain very favourable to the latter. Alternatively the process could be reversed — critical analysis of the letter could lead to the question 'what is he so angry about?' and this could lead into reconstruction of logistics/terrain and hence the whole predicament.[28]

It is also important, of course, that sources should not only be addressed appropriately but, where possible, checked for accuracy. Again it is a mistake to assume that young children cannot do this. For example, pictures of chain mail from the Bayeux Tapestry may be combined with photographs of chain-mail worn by the Vikings ('The Normans' Ancestors') and with a written description of Norman armour by someone who can never have seen the Bayeux Tapestry. All sources are found to tally.[29] The impact of such work will be lessened if the solutions are always presented along with the sources. Perhaps after some examples have been given, the children should have to work through the sources for themselves. In this example, the question could be posed 'how do we know that what the Bayeux Tapestry shows is true?', and the task could have been to select the corroborating sources from amongst a range of material of varying degrees of relevance to the question.

A key clue in selection would be *dating* of sources, and this needs further discussion, particularly in view of its frequent neglect in text books. If a picture is to be used as evidence for anything we must know when it was produced. As an example: Michael Foss's book *Chivalry* includes a reproduction of mounted knights entitled 'Charlemagne and his army march for Spain' (p. 37). It would be a grave error if this was taken, as by the unwary it might be, for an accurate representation of Carolingian cavalry. The picture dates from the twelfth century and the artist has drawn the arms and armour with which he is familiar. Foss in fact makes the relevant point very well. Not only does he give a full reference to the source in the list of references (pp. 247-48), but the caption adds 'From a twelfth-century manuscript'. Elsewhere he tellingly presents an illustration from an eleventh-century Bible showing the Israelites in full Norman armour, explaining that 'the artist of this Latin bible has portrayed biblical warfare according to eleventh-century practice'. Obviously, this treatment admirably introduces the point at issue, but textbooks commonly fail to do this and it should now be clear why failure to give the date or source of the materials used is so serious, for in the form of spurious authenticity, anachronism may be embraced and the possibility of a criticism of sources is foreclosed.

Guarding against anachronistic thinking is a skill which must be constantly practised and extended throughout historical study, for anachronism is an arch-enemy of understanding among adults and only history is prophylactic against it. The skills the primary children were broaching in the examples just discussed must be constantly practised and steadily deepened upon more and more complex contents so that, as fifth- or sixth-formers, they penetrate to and understand those past realities. Their *present* frame of reference, and their *present* attitudes and behaviour may thus be shaped by a past which actually happened.

## Enabling knowledge: empathy: imagination: context

If sources can lead to reconstruction only when they are critically appraised and when the right questions are put to them, this is not a matter of mechanically applying a check-list. The questions become meaningful only through enabling knowledge. As a very simple example consider what must already be known if reconstruction is to be facilitated by, or any sense made of, the 'Tyrone is a coward' passage. As a minimum a student must know who 'Tyrone' was, that a conflict between Irish and English was taking place — and so on.

The same need for enabling and underpinning knowledge holds for 'empathy' and 'imaginative inference'. As a rough approximation, empathising may be defined as 'standing in the shoes' of the historical personage one is studying.[30] But it is quite impossible to do this unless one has quite detailed knowledge of the circumstances in which he was in fact placed. To empathise with Cromwell at the siege of Drogheda is to see how the position looked to him, and to do this one must understand, inter alia, the insecurity of the revolution after the king's execution, the attitude of foreign powers, the strategic importance of Ireland and the direct threat brewing in Scotland. One must also have a 'backlog' of less specific but still relevant knowledge, such as the bitter memories at the 1641 rising — contemporaries did not, of course, know that the tales of massacre were greatly exaggerated — and the norms of seventeenth-century warfare. The horrors of the Thirty Years' War had only just ended. To put Drogheda into perspective it is appropriate to recall them. The sack of Frankfurt by the Swedes and of Magdeburg by the Imperial forces, while perhaps the worst events, differed only in degree from others. In the latter, at least three-quarters of the population were massacred and the town almost destroyed by fire. This means that, proportionately, Magdeburg suffered a disaster greater than that experienced by any city from aerial bombardment in the last war. The victorious Catholic general is reported to have observed that such an awful visitation of God had not been witnessed since the Romans under Titus destroyed Jerusalem.[31] This is how men of the time thought and spoke — which is not at all to assert that their motivation was purely (in either sense) religious. It makes it easier to empathise — not sympathise — with Cromwell's report to the House of Commons on the capture of Drogheda — a 'righteous judgement of God upon these barbarous wretches who have imbrued their hands in so much innocent blood'. Cromwell lived closer than we do to the fires of Smithfield.

To urge all this is in no way to excuse — or to blame. It is to explain — and this is the historian's job. To empathise is to reconstruct a perception of reality (in this case, Cromwell's) and this is a cognitive, rather than an emotional, achievement, for it depends upon knowledge rather than feeling. Of course, it also involves imagination since only *traces* of the past remain, a facility for going beyond the knowledge they can yield is the only thing that can make historical accounts complete. But imagination in history is no 'fancy free — let's imagine — let's pretend' exercise in 'making it up', but a question of insights into what was possible and probable in the light, first of what is known from sources and enabling background knowledge about the particular event or process in question, and second, increasingly as the children mature and grow in experience, of that appropriate general frame of reference whose importance and acquisition has been identified as the prime benefit bestowed by the study of history. Thus, while imagination as well as its close relative, empathy, is needed in history, this does not weaken the claim that reconstruction is a cognitive achievement, for historical imagination, no less than empathy, is knowledge-based.[32]

The fourth characteristic of historical reconstruction discriminated above was *context.* This needs little more direct discussion since it is only another name for the 'enabling knowledge', shown to be crucial for adequate use of sources and for the achievement of empathy and imaginative inference. However, the importance of context has another crucial aspect. It is a necessary complement to the use of *hindsight*. One can only misunderstand Luther's action in nailing his 95 theses to the church door at Wittenberg if one views it as an unprecedented act of uncompromising defiance. If based on such a view, the conventional choice of 31 October 1517 as 'Reformation Day' is an illicit use of hindsight. For, of course, to publish argumentative theses was a normal way of inviting dispute; churches were normal places to issue such invitations; Luther had, at that time, no thought of provoking a final breach with Rome; and it is by no means certain that such a break was caused by, or inevitable after, his action. To fail to recognise all this and to plump for '1517-Reformation' is to fail to 'empathise' or to 'reconstruct imaginatively', because it misrepresents Luther's actual position and intentions; it is to use our knowledge of what came after to impose an over-tidy, teleological pattern upon the past and radically to distort its meaning. This point is particularly important in view of the crucial role ascribed to hindsight when historical explanation was discussed in the first chapter. Without hindsight, explanation and understanding cannot be had at all, for there is then no way of discriminating significant events from those which had no important consequences: yet to use it seems to invite vicious anachronism and misunderstanding. The remedy, however is clear. It lies in reconstructing events in context and through the enabling knowledge which context affords. This provides the necessary and sufficient means for hindsight to be correctly employed, for the significance of an event only becomes clear after it is correctly known. And in teaching children we may be helped by the fact that they are shielded from the possible distorting effect of hindsight by their ignorance. They do not know what the outcome was. It should, therefore, be a straightforward, though not a simple, matter to reconstruct an event as it was by creating its context.[33] Understanding of the event cannot, admittedly, be complete until its outcome and consequences are known. That will come later. For the time the reconstruction of the event in itself can provide the means for a subsequent correct understanding of its consequences.

## Context and teaching

The stress upon context has also a crucial implication for teaching. It shows why all teaching and learning cannot be 'Know-howful'. For no matter with what sources one starts, enabling knowledge is necessary for their proper use and if that knowledge has to be acquired know-howfully, — i.e. from sources — those sources will require, in their turn, enabling knowledge for this use — which in *its* turn must be 'know-howfully' acquired through sources, which . . . If the futility of infinite regression is to be avoided, then enabling knowledge must be otherwise acquired. It is fortunate that this logical impediment exists because, of course, shortage of time would in practice rule out learning everything 'know-howfully' even if it were in principle possible. A balance, then, is needed between 'know-that' and 'know-how'.

Where are criteria for such a balance to be found? The onus here is on the teacher and/or the textbook. The logical inadmissibility of dogmatic and assertive teaching resting on *mere* authority has been shown elsewhere:[34] the impossibility of doing everything from sources has just been indicated. The need is, therefore, to identify some other form of expository teaching which will rightfully fill the gap by being epistemologically acceptable. The answer is not far to seek. The teacher must not only provide context by a narrative, but must show why it is accepted, and acceptable, as true. That is, he must frequently show and discuss the grounds upon which his story rests and the procedures of which it is the outcome: and these must tally with the sorts of procedure and ground that the pupil is led to employ and accept when he works with sources.

In short, the two operations — the children actually working with sources and being 'programmed' with the context needed to undertake such work — are reciprocal and closely related. Indeed, they are mediated by a third. Every so often the teacher may embark on a summary and recapitulatory lesson when, in more or less straight narrative, he pulls together the context-building account which has been fruitfully interrupted by frequent demonstrations and discussions of criteria, procedures and evidence as the story unfolds. Depending on their age, there may be a good case for the pupils making a permanent record of the summary before engaging in the detailed source-based work of the next 'patch' for which they are now prepared. It should be obvious that the three processes may overlap: but all three should be distinctly served. The main difference is that the teacher's use of sources and evidence is to show the children the justice of an account he already knows to be valid. The use is thus summary; the children, on the other hand, have to reverse the process. Having (sometimes) checked the sources for reliability they must then be prompted into making a reconstruction from them. Here again the teacher's role is crucial, for he has to deflect them from superficial details ('how many cows did O'Neil take in this prey?', 'to whom was the captured castle given by O'Neil?') to the silent, hidden but true significance of the passages (why all this fuss about cows? what does this suggest to us about the Irish way of life and economy?).

It should be clear that this learning process may also contribute to building 'frames of reference'. For example, in his 'enabling exposition' leading into a study of the Nine Years' War the teacher can hardly fail, in commenting on the English presence in Ireland, to say something of its rationale; similarly, in using sources the pupils can be led to check, confirm or modify the view he has given them of that rationale, and thus to broach the questions of security, strategic importance and, perhaps, 'national interest'. This is why the 'enabling knowledge' must include a schematised sketch of the international situation in the late sixteenth century.[35] The children might be asked to jot down, say, six points which struck them as in any way interesting or important during their study of the sources. First, this can give the teacher priceless insight into the learning process. No adult can comprehensively predict what *is* 'important' to children, and to find out not only makes our teaching more relevant to them, but may indicate genuinely important points which we had overlooked. When their suggestions are discussed, their ideas of 'importance' can be sharpened, and, specifically, building mature frames of references can begin. For example, one ten year-old having learned from an

Irish source that the Pope was involved in political and military machinations, asked 'How come the Pope, a man of peace, is joining in?'. It is scarcely too much to say that, if persevered in, this process would be a growing point of mental life, a movement towards a mature and sophisticated view of 'how things are' which will result in sixthformers being able significantly to discuss and evaluate inter alia the complexities of the Anglo-Irish Treaty negotiations.

It is easy to see how these examples imply a highly co-ordinated course which continues for a long time and where the same principles and concepts are repeatedly encountered in increasingly complex form.[36] To build the frames of reference such a continuous experience is needed, for it can finally be achieved only by the most mature pupils, and only then as a result of protracted and regular practice. In their fully developed form the concepts, principles and procedures involved are abstract and difficult. 'Balance of power', 'national interest', 'sovereignty', to give only political examples, can be truly understood only by a very small minority of pupils unless their final form is underpinned and prepared by long experience of many concrete or palpable examples. Without such experience the terms, if learned at all, remain mere empty mouthings. Indeed, it might be thought that they are less important than understanding the examples. But is this not a distinction without a difference? It is a mistake to suppose that no use of the terms is to be made until all instances of them have been experienced. What could constitute 'all'? On the contrary, the two processes go on together, and provisional and preliminary uses of the terms accompany the practical work from an early stage. The meaning and application of, at any rate some of, the terms is thus gradually developed. The terms are vital, for understanding cannot be comprehensive and complete until a concept has become 'disembodied', so to speak — not in the sense of being unrelated to the examples in which it has been experienced, but, on the contrary, by encompassing and synthesising them all. And that 'disembodiment' requires a definite symbol to give it the precision which enables it to be applied.

The thrust of the whole argument has implications for content to be studied as well as for length of study. For analogies can only be found among events which actually are analogous. Whatever present issues are judged to be important, it is the record of the same type of past event which should figure in history courses if relevant analogies are to be drawn and the appropriate frame(s) of reference constructed. The question as to what history it is important to teach is not, therefore, as difficult, nor answers to it as arbitrary, as might at first seem. It is not really a question about *history* at all, but about what *things* are important in our contemporary life. Of course, there would hardly be unanimity about this, but general consensus would surely select the big social, economic[37] and political questions of the day — big in the sense of being heavy with actual or potential consequences for people in general. The main role of history, then, is to provide enabling knowledge and frame of reference for these important matters so that present behaviour is coloured and shaped by assumptions which are realistic because they are rooted in a past which actually happened, not tendentious travesties or fictions in fancy dress.

It must be admitted that this runs counter to much of the prevailing orthodoxy which enshrines 'interest' and 'enquiry' as the twin touchstones of validity for history courses. Both of these began as healthy correctives to indefensible aspects of much traditional history teaching, but have become distorted and exaggerated. The fact that pupils happen to be interested in something is, in itself, no reason to choose it for study — unless it is assumed that whatever pupils happen to fancy is what they ought to do. But in that case we may as well give up — indeed, we will already have given up — thinking about doing things for *reasons* at all. The Eurovision Song Contest, or the European Cup competition may be vastly more interesting to many, if not most, pupils than understanding events in, say, the Middle East: but that only shows the utter inadequacy of 'interest' as the main criterion of education. And this is no unsubstantiated prejudice or value judgment. Nothing turns on, and no consequences of any significance follow from, the outcome of the two contests, whereas the practical behaviour flowing from lack of an informed understanding of the Middle East problem may be, literally, a matter of life or death for half the world. The contests have to be categorised as 'trivial', the Middle East as 'important'. Indeed, it is from such exemplars that those concepts themselves are obtained and developed. The twin dangers of public ignorance of such matters are that it may remove any check upon the actions of government because people feel apathetic or inhibited by incompetence or that alternatively governments may be driven by uninformed popular passion into acts of folly which are counter-productive to what it is actually desired, and important, to achieve.[38] A well-informed public opinion is indispensable on any democratic assumption, or any prudential consideration. There can, therefore, be no question as to which *sorts* of issue should figure in the curriculum, or that all pupils should study them. Because of history's central role in providing specific enabling knowledge and frame of reference for such important matters this carries the strongest implications for the content of the history curriculum, and entails that history must be a compulsory 'core' subject for all pupils.

It may be felt that the argument has been caricatured by choosing examples so trivial that no one would actually think of including them; but they are not much more trivial than the sort of topic not infrequently studied because of the indiscriminate vogue for 'enquiry' among incautious and unreflecting advocates of the 'new' history, whose attitude may be colloquially summed up as 'content doesn't matter'; for, so it is held, it is the skills of enquiry which are important, since these will provide the children with the tools and means to find out whatever information they may need in the future. The worrying implication is that these skills are seen as quite general, learnable on almost any content, and, insofar as they are learned, applicable to, and adequate for, any other. That this is an error should be clear from the earlier stress on context and frames of reference as imperative for significant enquiries: the one consists of, and the other is built from, *particular* content. 'Content doesn't matter' is thus the 'transfer of training' fallacy in modern dress. The bizarre idea that one learns to think in any adequate way about the Middle East, or super-power rivalry, or the problems of inner cities, by studying the history of the local football team or aspects in the development of the local dye works, or discovering what the Romans may have worn beneath their togas needs to be seen for the nonsense it is.

Even the skills of enquiry themselves are not sufficiently uniform for the procedures used in any of the 'trivial' triad to be adequate for any of the 'serious' one. Only at the simplest level of enquiry, where all, or nearly all, that is at stake is observing, and learning to ensure conformity with, broad and basic logical requirements such as consistency would they transfer. And this points up a valid though limited role for enquiries into 'trivial' matters. There is no reason why these should not figure in the work of the younger pupils since procedures have to be gradually learned. Even so, it is an error to suppose that 'serious' topics cannot be tackled with and by young children,[39] and the greater carry-over between such studies and those which the children must later undertake, if the prime object of studying history is to be attained, indicates that the use of 'trivial' ones should be sparing. This slight qualification of the embargo upon non-serious content must be accompanied by a clarification of 'interest' and a more precise specification of 'trivial'. The two must not be regarded as linked. If they are, we speedily return to the days of 'good old grinding' when anything pupils found attractive was automatically suspect as a primrose path of dalliance. On the contrary, if learning is to occur, the work must by all means be as interesting as possible. But this consideration cannot determine choice of content — 'making it interesting' is mainly a question for methodology. And, of course, the linkage is quite wrong in its tacit assumption that serious content must be a steep and thorny road.

Economic social and political content with (some) appropriate source-based work can be made attractive to 10 and 12 year olds[40] and, of course, content which is in itself trivial can sometimes lead into serious themes. If the study of the local football team is merely that, then 'trivial' is just what it is: but if, as may be the case, study of the club's origin and development is used to motivate reconstruction of a past reality through raising issues such as public health, housing conditions, law and order, or the social significance of the club in a grossly deprived community, then a most valuable enterprise is undertaken: for it is contributing to the frame of reference through which important present problems, such as football hooliganism, may perhaps be understood. Similarly if the local dye-works is examined in the context of the Industrial Revolution and used as a palpable exemplar to bring understanding to that wider reality, then it can be a most valuable, though still subsidiary, study. Spontaneous and local interests are, therefore, by no means to be excluded — provided that they do in practice lead on to the sort of serious issues mentioned.

With these qualifications and clarifications the main point stands, and may be restated. History should have a substantial place in the 'core' curriculum, compulsory for all pupils throughout their school lives. The justification for this demand prescribes the sort of 'important' content just described, for only study of this can contribute to the development in our citizens-to-be of the sort of understanding described in earlier chapters which it is a matter almost of life and death that they should have. Of course, history has other aspects and roles. It can also be the source of a range of hobbies which some people find fascinating and there is no reason why optional time on a voluntary basis — say, the after-hours history club — should not concern itself with them. This work has nothing to say about such optional extras. It is concerned with history in the core curriculum, and there can be no case for compelling all pupils to study things merely because some of them find these rewarding — things whose study cannot secure the capital benefit which is the justification for using compulsion in the first place. History will neither command nor deserve respect from our colleagues, our pupils or the public at large if it claims to provide benefits which, through wrongful choice of content, it palpably does not secure, or if, abandoning all such claims, it brazenly defends studies whose content and outcome are manifestly, and admittedly, trivial on no better ground than that (some) pupils happen to 'get something (unspecified) out of them'.

The justification of history as a core, compulsory subject thus requires that the content shall consist of political, social and economic affairs. It is in these areas that the development of frames of reference by analysis is imperative. Provided this is done, the choice of period(s) for study might seem unimportant. However, other criteria carry the matter further. First to understand the present world, facts are needed as well as analogies and the recent past is likely to contain most of the most relevant ones. It would seem to follow that modern history should be the chosen content. Yet, as against this modernist 'tilt', two points must be made. First, one of the more valuable things history has to offer is *contrast*. There is a very strong tendency to view the values and assumptions of our own society as given or inevitable and it is, consequently, very difficult to subject them to much needed critical appraisal. The historical record of how and why they became what they are is an invaluable aid here (they cannot be given if they have evolved), but so is the study of other societies whose values were significantly different — and these, almost inevitably, will be remote from us in time. History can aid critical review by showing that things do not have to be as they are — we can be sure of that, because they have been different. So far from contradicting the main aim of building 'frames of reference', the study of contrast aids it. For difference is only ever partial. Amidst all the dissimilarities between our own world and those (say) of the Middle Ages or Ancient Greece are found elements of similarity which echo our own experience and without which we could not understand at all. The words Thucydides put into the mouths of the Athenian ambassadors to Melos are but an unusually bleak and lucid enunciation of truths which, with modifications, structure foreign policy in our world too. Analysing and accounting for the modifications is a large part of what it is to draw analogies and build appropriate frames of reference. Moreover, bearing in mind the inductive nature of the process of analogy, the dangers of induction need to be guarded against by not basing it on a very narrow range of experience, as would be the case if study were confined to modern history.

One crucial implication of all that has been said is that the 'patch' approach to teaching is virtually prescribed. Given that a range of periods has to be studied in order to secure necessary contrast and to have a range of comparisons wide enough to provide analogy with a secure footing, and given that, in consequence, each period chosen must be studied in depth and detail, including considerable amounts of source-based work, the time factor alone rules out any other approach. Two more things need to be said. First, whatever 'set' of 'patches' is chosen must be clearly co-ordinated so as to yield continuous experience of the principles, concepts and procedures. For example, within the limits imposed by faithfulness to the periods studied, analogy must be stressed. As a crude first approximation, 'history repeats itself' will do — but this must be soon and thoroughly developed by probing the modifications forced upon such a generalisation by each new 'patch' studied.

Even with the enabling context for each patch supplied in narrative form, it is inevitable that gaps will be left in the pupils' knowledge if we are thinking in terms of conventional chronological coverage: but such coverage always was a quite unrealistic aim — a sure recipe for '1066 and all that'. Moreover, it was itself arbitrarily selective. It was only for British (or, more likely, English) history that coverage was even attempted. What of the rest of Europe? What of extra-European civilisations? This basis of selection reinforces the argument of the present work, for it clearly, if tacitly, reflects a shared concern with what is thought most relevant to our present. It is claimed that, as the opening of this chapter acknowledged, chronological coverage rarely results in that vital conceptual growth and grasp that only history can provide. Properly co-ordinated, a 'patch' approach can do so.

# ●Notes●

**1.** A.C. Danto, *Analytical Philosophy of History* (Cambridge, 1968), p. 149.
**2.** The *dangers* of 'hindsight' will also be considered.
**3.** Danto, *op cit*, p. 122.
**4.** Danto, *op cit*, p. 97.
**5.** C. Hill, *Puritanism and Revolution* (Mercury, 1958), p. 143.
**6.** G.R. Elton, *The Practice of History* (Fontana, 1967), pp. 23-24.
**7.** On this point, see Danto, *op cit*, p. 99 and (especially) p. 100: 'One has access to the past only through inference and to make such inferences requires, or pre-supposes, certain theoretical sentences, whether made explicit or not, which connect present evidence with past fact'. The 'theoretical sentences' express just the frame of reference or set of assumptions argued for here.
**8.** C.G. Hempel, 'The function of general laws in history', *Journal of Philosophy*, Vol XXXIX, 1942.
**9.** For an account of continuities in Russian defence policy caused by the sense of technological inferiority see W.C. Clemens, 'Nicholas II to Salt 2', *International Affairs*, July 1973, pp. 385-401.
**10.** On this point, see P.J. Lee, 'Why Learn History?' in A.K. Dickinson, P.J. Lee and P.J. Rogers (eds),

*Learning History* (Heinemann, 1984), pp. 1-19.
**11.** J.H. Hexter, *Reappraisals in History* (Longman, 1967), p. 8.
**12.** G. Kitson Clark, *The Critical Historian* (Heinemann, 1967), p. 27.
**13.** K.R. Popper, *The Poverty of Historicism* (Routledge, 1957), p. 145.
**14.** C.G. Burnham, 'Czechoslovakia: Thirty Years after Munich', *Yearbook of World Affairs*, Summer 1969, pp. 53-81.
**15.** Anon., *On events in Czechoslovakia* (Moscow, obtained from Soviet Embassy in London).
**16.** For a full account of this experiment see P.J. Rogers, 'History and Political Education', *Teaching Politics*, May 1979, Vol 8, no. 2, pp. 153-169.
**17.** *Cambridge Economic History of Europe*, Vol VIII, part 2, p. 160.
**18.** In particular, the practical and pragmatic process such study reveals is a salutary solvent to notions of a higher purpose unfolding itself, of a steady march towards progress and enlightenment. One might almost as well credit medieval barons with democratic (or, at least, representative) intentions — Disraeli, in *Sybil*, almost did so!
**19.** On all this see T.O. Lloyd,

*Empire to Welfare State* (Oxford, 1970), pp. 42-45.

**20.** J.B. Conant, *On understanding science* (Mentor, 1951), pp. 27-32.

**21.** E.H. Hutten, *The ideas of Physics* (Oliver and Boyd, 1967), pp. v, 3-7.

**22.** As further examples, see for economics 'The past as a frame of reference' in C. Portal (ed), *History and History Teaching* (Falmer, in press). For art, see P.J. Rogers, 'History' in K. Dixon (ed), *Philosophy of Education and the Curriculum* (Pergamon, 1972), especially pp. 79-82.

**23.** This is the objection to the 'lines of development' approach — that some theme, say transport, is selected, and its development charted as if it was a perfectly autonomous matter. 'Costume (or houses) through the ages' are popular examples of the same error.

**24.** L. Stenhouse, 'The Humanities Curriculum Project', *Journal of Curriculum Studies*, 1969, Vol 1, no. 1.

**25.** P.J. Rogers, *The New History: theory into practice* (Historical Association, 1979), chapter one.

**26.** For a critique of textbooks which concludes that a good one is almost impossible to write see P.J. Rogers, 'Some thoughts on the textbook', *Teaching History*, October 1981, no. 31, pp. 28-30.

**27.** See P.J. Rogers, *The New History*, chapters four and five.

**28.** See P.J. Rogers, *The New History*, pp. 41-42.

**29.** L. Yeatman, *The Normans in Europe*, The Way It Was series, (Chambers, 1976).

**30.** For an extended discussion of 'empathy' see D. Shemilt, 'Beauty and the Philosopher' in Dickinson, Lee and Rogers (eds), *op cit*, pp. 39-84.

**31.** On all this see G. Parker, *Europe in Crisis, 1598-1648* (Fontana, 1979), p. 221.

**32.** For an extended discussion of imagination in history see P.J. Lee in Dickinson, Lee and Rogers (eds), *op cit*, pp. 85-116.

**33.** The stress laid in this section (and elsewhere) upon the event 'as it was' should make it clear that what is argued for is in no sense the 'practical' history against which Professor Oakeshott warns us. True, our motive for making history compulsory for all pupils is ulterior in that it is not 'for its own sake' but so that they may better understand a state of affairs subsequent to it (the present); but historical study can only secure this end if history is studied *as if* for its own sake — that is, with fullest rigour and by all appropriate procedures. For extended discussions of this point see Rogers, 'History', in Dixon (ed), *op cit*, pp. 108-110.

**34.** See P.J. Rogers, *The New History*, chapter one.

**35.** See P.J. Rogers, *The New History*, chapter five.

**36.** J.S. Bruner, *The Process of Education* (Harvard, 1959), p. 29. For the 'Spiral curriculum' applied to history see P.J. Rogers, *The New History*, chapter four.

**37.** For a brief discussion of the relation between history and economics see P.J. Rogers, 'The past as a frame of reference' in Portal (ed), *op cit*.

**38.** For an extended example see P.J. Rogers, 'The past as a frame of reference' in Portal (ed), *op cit*.

**39.** In particular it is a mistake to imagine that political topics cannot be broached — of course, in very scaled-down form, and with very carefully chosen content — with younger children. See Rogers, *The New History*.

**40.** See note 39.